GW00507370

Further Pra
Monetary Reform – *M*

*"As one would expect from the a
Reform - Making it Happen!' makes a stimulating addition to a
debate about one of the most important, but as yet too
inadequately understood, changes required to the financial system
globally."* **Colin Hines**
Author, *Localisation - a global manifesto*

*"I'm happy to see two good ideas merge into a single strategy.
Wishing you both the best of success!"* **Bernard Lietaer**
Author, *The Future of Money*

*"This is a brilliant treatment of a question which has never been
so urgent. James Robertson tackles the issue which underpins
everything else we are concerned about and, as always, he does it
with clarity and panache."* **George Monbiot**
Author, *The Age of Consent*

*"A wonderfully clear exposition of two very important ideas,
which could be of mutual assistance although neither needs the
other for support."* **Richard Douthwaite**
Author, *The Growth Illusion* and *Short Circuit*

*"This proposal of Robertson and Bunzl will create a new starting
point for the discussion of realistic and practical ways and means
to create the necessary changes for a more just global society.
The combination of approaches to monetary reform and
democratic-decision making across national boundaries could
offer a win-win solution for both. It will resonate positively with a
growing number of Cultural Creatives around the globe, aiming
to promote the changes necessary for a more just and democratic
world order."* **Prof. Dr. Margrit Kennedy**
Author, *Interest and Inflation Free Money*

1

About the Authors

James Robertson

After studying classics, history and philosophy at Oxford University, he worked in government in London. He was on Prime Minister Harold Macmillan's staff for his "Wind of Change" tour of Africa in 1960, and then spent three years in the Cabinet Office. Then he became director of inter-bank research for the big British banks.

Since the 1970s he has been an independent writer and speaker. In the mid-1980s he was a prominent co-founder of The Other Economic Summit (TOES) and the New Economics Foundation.

His best known book is probably *The Sane Alternative* (1978, 1983). Recent books and reports include:
- *Transforming Economic Life* (for UK Schumacher Society), 1998;
- *The New Economics of Sustainable Development: A briefing for policy-makers* (for the European Commission), 1999 -
  a) Kogan Page, London,
  b) Editions Apogée, Paris (as *Changer d'Economie: ou la Nouvelle Economie du Développement Durable*),
  c) Office for Official Publications of the European Communities, Luxembourg.
- *Creating New Money: A Monetary Reform for the Information Age,* with Professor Joseph Huber (for New Economics Foundation), 2000.

In October 2003, at the XXIX annual conference of the Pio Manzu Research Centre, Rimini, Italy (closely associated with the UN), he was awarded a gold medal for his "remarkable contribution to the promotion of a new economics grounded in social and spiritual values" over the past 25 years. In a session on "Sharing Limited Resources And A Change Of Course" he gave a paper on "The Role of Money and Finance: Changing a Central Part of the Problem into a Central Part of the Solution".

E-mail: robertson@tp2000.demon.co.uk
Web: www.ecoplan.org/tp2000

John Bunzl

After studying modern languages and business studies in France Switzerland and Italy, John pursued a commercial career trading in raw materials for the paper industry and, more recently, in the sale of specialised technical papers primarily to the filtration, abrasives and medical supplies industries.

Having had only a passing interest in international affairs and in the thinking of E.F. Schumacher, in 1998 the idea for Simultaneous Policy suddenly occurred to him as a potential means for removing the barriers which prevent many of today's global problems from being solved. In 2000 he founded the International Simultaneous Policy Organisation (ISPO) and launched the Simultaneous Policy (SP) campaign. In 2001, he set out the campaign in his first book of the same name. The SP campaign has since steadily been gathering increasing attention, recognition and support amongst citizens, activists, non-governmental organisations, politicians, business people and many others.

He is a company director and is married with three children.

E-mail: jbunzl@simpol.org
Web: www.simpol.org

Monetary Reform
– *Making it Happen!*

James Robertson

and

John Bunzl

International Simultaneous Policy Organisation
London

First published in 2003
by the International Simultaneous Policy Organisation
P.O. Box 26547, London, SE3 7YT, UK.
www.simpol.org   info@simpol.org
Tel. +44 (0)20-8464 4141

A catalogue record for this publication is available from the
British Library

ISBN 0-9546727-0-4

Cover design by Lloyd Allen, Orbit Graphic Communication

Printed by Antony Rowe Ltd., Chippenham, Wiltshire, UK.

Monetary Reform
– Making it Happen!

CONTENTS

SUMMARY

By James Robertson and John Bunzl

Pressures for a new political economy are becoming stronger as worldwide protest against the present form of globalisation, coupled with anxiety about American 'imperialism', continues to grow. The new political economy will need to combine *economic efficiency* to enable people to meet their needs with *justice* between people and *sparing use* of natural resources ('environmental sustainability'). It will require changes in today's economic and political institutions - particularly those concerned with the workings of money and finance.

These changes will have a vital international dimension. As a practical example of how it might be necessary to handle this, this book explores the possible scope for linking two proposals that have come forward in Britain during the past three years. One is for monetary reform as proposed by Joseph Huber and James Robertson in 2000.[1] The other is for Simultaneous Policy, as proposed by John Bunzl in 2001.[2] Simultaneous Policy is a general strategic approach, aiming to smooth the path to desirable reforms through their simultaneous implementation by enough countries to overcome the objection that a single country implementing them would risk capital flight and damage to its international competitiveness.

---

[1] Joseph Huber and James Robertson, *Creating New Money: A Monetary Reform for the Information Age,* New Economics Foundation, London, 2000 - summarised in *World Review,* Vol 4, No 2, New European Publications, London, 2000.

[2] John M. Bunzl, *The Simultaneous Policy: An Insider's Guide to Saving Humanity and the Planet,* New European Publications, London, 2001 - summarised in *World Review,* Vol 5, No 1, 2002.

The first two chapters on monetary reform are by James Robertson. Although much of the detail in them refers to Britain, the same outline applies broadly to other countries too.

The historical perspective in Chapter 1 brings out some of the parallels between the aims of monetary reform in the 19th century and now, and some of the differences between that time and ours. It suggests that the historical evolution of the monetary system between then and now points to the Huber/Robertson proposal as the next step forward.

It also points out that a key difference between then and now is that monetary reform must be dealt with today in an international context. Another difference is that now public awareness is becoming widespread that big changes in the monetary and financial system are needed. People's aspirations for a greener, juster, more people-centred way of life, a new direction of more peaceful progress, and a new consciousness about our place in the planet, are growing. But recognition is also growing that those aspirations cannot be fulfilled, so long as the perverse incentives and compulsions of the present money system shape how we actually live.

Chapter 2 summarises the proposal for monetary reform published in *Creating New Money*, and brings out its international as well as its national significance. It notes some of the main obstacles to it that have become apparent and some of the objections that have been made to it, including those based on the risk of damage to a national economy's international competitiveness.

Chapter 3 is written by John Bunzl. It introduces the Simultaneous Policy approach and explains its potential relevance to monetary reform proposals such as *Creating New Money*, as well as to other reforms advocated by global justice campaigners and non-governmental organisations (NGOs). It outlines in more detail the obstacles to the implementation of monetary reform likely to arise from the reaction of global markets, and it explains how Simultaneous Policy could potentially overcome them. Specific arguments in favour of the Simultaneous Policy approach are discussed as well as its potential disadvantages and responses to them.

Chapter 4 re-emphasises the importance of an international campaign for monetary reform. It will probably be based initially on non-governmental organisations (NGOs) mobilising citizens' interests worldwide, bringing in small businesses and other sectors inadequately served by the present money system, and then spreading to growing numbers of mainstream politicians, political parties, government officials, financial experts and economists.

That chapter and the book conclude with some practical suggestions about what can be done to promote monetary reform by its supporters

- in their own nation,
- co-operating internationally,
- and provisionally adopting the Simultaneous Policy.

Acknowledgments

We acknowledge with sincere thanks a grant from the Greening the North Fund and from Mrs. G.J. Bunzl towards the costs of printing and distributing this book. We are also very grateful to Brian Wills and Colin Hines, both of whom gave valuable assistance on various matters of detail.

CHAPTER 1

A HISTORICAL PERSPECTIVE
By James Robertson

This chapter outlines, in a historical perspective, the global context today for the proposal for mainstream monetary reform put forward by Joseph Huber and myself in *Creating New Money*.[3] Briefly, that proposal is that new official-currency money (pounds, euros, dollars, etc) should no longer be created by commercial banks as profit-making loans to their customers. It should be created by central monetary authorities (today's central banks) which should give it as debt-free public revenue to their governments to spend into circulation for public purposes.

The first half of the 19th century was a time of profound economic and political change in Britain. The early 21st century is a comparable period. Although the changes we face are now worldwide, what happened in early 19th-century Britain can help us to understand some of the important challenges we face. Monetary reform is one of them.

Thomas Attwood was an early 19th-century monetary and political reformer.[4] He played a vital part in one of the great events of his time.

---

[3] Joseph Huber and James Robertson, *Creating New Money: A monetary reform for the information age*, New Economics Foundation, London, 2000.

[4] I am drawing here on my Thomas Attwood memorial lecture in B M Insight, Issue 5, 2003 - the Journal of the British Midland Institute and Library, 9 Margaret Street, Birmingham B3 3BS. Fuller information about him will be found in D.J. Moss, *Thomas Attwood: the biography of a radical*, McGill-Queen's University Press, Montreal & London, 1990, and Joseph Hunt, *Thomas Attwood: Hales Owen's Forgotten Genius,* B M Insight, Issue 4 2001.

As a family banker aged 29, in 1812 he had made his mark with the manufacturers and artisans of Birmingham by leading a political campaign on their behalf against the monopoly enjoyed by the East India Company and other British Government restrictions on overseas trade. That campaign confirmed that the urban manufacturing classes - the business owners and the working people - who had sprung from the industrial revolution and were unrepresented in parliament, could work together in support of their common interests; and that those interests conflicted with the agricultural, commercial and financial interests of the rural land-owning classes whose representatives still monopolised parliament and government. Attwood was radicalised by his experience of what we would now call "the Westminster village". He wrote to his wife in 1812, "Such a set of feeble mortals as the members of both Houses are, I never did expect to meet in this world. The best among them are scarce equal to the worst in Birmingham". For the next ten or fifteen years his energies were directed to monetary reform, but then he was to play a key part in the successful passage of the great parliamentary Reform Act of 1832.

The transformation of the economy by the industrial revolution was straining existing monetary institutions and theories. In 1797 the effects of the Napoleonic Wars had driven the Bank of England off the gold standard; the exchangeability of its banknotes for gold sovereigns had been suspended. Between 1810 and 1819 Attwood campaigned, eventually unsuccessfully, against the parliamentary "Bullion Report" which recommended that the number and value of banknotes in circulation should be reduced and their exchangeability for gold should be restored.

Attwood and his colleagues in the "Paper Money" school were, in effect, calling for money to be permanently *redefined* to include paper banknotes as well as gold coins and bullion. Today this redefinition has been long accepted. Banknotes are recognised, along with coins, to be "cash". Like coins they are now issued debt-free by an agency of the state, the Bank of England. Although British banknotes still say "I promise to pay... ", that is a meaningless survival from past history. Banknotes now are not just credit notes. Everyone knows they are cash.[5]

The challenge we face is similar to Attwood's. But our definition of money should now extend to include, not just banknotes as well as coin, but also the electronic bank-created money in our current bank accounts. Although some people with pretensions to knowledge of these things say that that is something distinct from money, called credit, it is now clearly recognised to be money, directly and immediately available for spending.[6] That commercial banks still create this official-currency money for private-sector profit has become a glaring anachronism.

As pressure grew for parliamentary reform in the 1820s Attwood recognised that monetary reformers would have to work together with campaigners for other radical causes. One of these was the campaign to repeal the Corn Laws, which imposed a tariff on imported grain and so protected agricultural profits and imposed dearer food on urban working people. In 1829 Attwood succeeded in bringing these various campaigning groups together under the banner of the Birmingham Political Union for the Protection of Public Rights, a new "general political union between the lower and middle classes of the people". Its first priority was to campaign for reform of the House of Commons, which had become, in Attwood's words, "the seat of ignorance, imbecility and indifference", filled by people who specialised in

---

[5] The Bank Charter Act of 1844 eventually resulted in a Bank of England monopoly of the banknote issue in England and Wales. Scottish and Northern Irish banks still issue their own banknotes, but these must be backed by Bank of England notes. However, the number and value of the banknotes issued are simply what is needed to meet the convenience of the public. They play no part in controlling the total value of the money supply. That is done by regulating interest rates, to control demand for the non-cash, bank-account money created by commercial banks and issued into their customers' accounts as interest-bearing loans.

[6] Today's official monetary statistics accept this, but raise a different problem. They contain alternative definitions of the money stock, based on confusing aggregates called M0, M1, M2, M3, M3 extended, M4, and so on. These are part of the veil of mystery which shrouds the workings of the money system even in "democratic" countries. The reform we are discussing will replace them with one clear definition of money, M.

the pursuit of power, influence and corruption. For the time being Attwood subordinated the cause of monetary reform to the cause of parliamentary reform.

As the Birmingham Political Union under his leadership spearheaded the parliamentary reform campaign, similar political unions spread all over the country. Huge demonstrations and marches to London were held. Attwood proved able not only to bring diverse political groups together but also to combine radical rhetoric with keeping his supporters on the path of "Peace, Law and Order" - so that, as John Stuart Mill put it later, they "should appear ready to break out into outrage, without actually breaking out".

The "anti-globalisation" demonstrations of recent years in cities like Seattle, Geneva and Washington may not precisely fit that description. But they have helped to focus attention on the case for reforming the institutions of the world's political economy and changing the path of world development being imposed by "the Washington Consensus". Although they have not been reported by the media as offering constructive alternatives to that path, they may have helped to prepare the world for them. Future historians will be the judges of that.

In June 1832 after the Reform Act had finally been passed Attwood was recognised to have been principally responsible for that historic achievement.[7] He was made a Freeman of the City of London and returned home to Birmingham at the head of a "march of triumph" - a growing procession of working people carrying banners proclaiming "Attwood and Liberty". He was at the peak of recognition and popularity, in Birmingham and throughout the country.

By 1833, he was in Parliament, as the first of the two Birmingham MPs in the new House of Commons elected after the Reform Act. But he bored his fellow MPs with lengthy expositions of

---

[7] e.g. by Attwood's contemporary, George Grote, whose name classics students will remember as a historian of Greece.

monetary theory. By 1834 they were impatient with him. In 1837 he pronounced them to be "as ignorant as asses and obstinate as hogs". He resigned from Parliament in 1839. Meanwhile, the new Bank of England representative in Birmingham described his ideas about currency reform as "ingenious" but "lamentably wrong". Economists called him a monomaniac, and the description stuck. Some years later banknotes (paper money) were recognised to be real money, and commercial banks were no longer allowed to create money by issuing them. But it was not until 1931 that Britain finally came off the gold standard, and not until 1973 that the USA did.

Today's Situation Compared with Early 19th Century Britain

The early 19th century was a time of great economic and social and political change in Britain. The American and French revolutions of 1776 and 1789 had inflamed political hopes and fears, and these had continued to smoulder during the Napoleonic Wars. At the same time, the industrial revolution had led to huge economic and social upheavals, and the institutions of society had been slow to adapt to them. The urban middle and working classes of Britain were ripe for mobilisation as a powerful force for change. It was against that background that Attwood and others like him strove for monetary and political reform in Britain.

By contrast, the big economic and political and environmental issues affecting our lives today are global in their reach. The adaptations and reforms we need are global, as well as national and local. We have learned that "Think globally, act locally" is not enough. Without changes at supranational levels, institutions which wield economic and political power today - the International Monetary Fund, World Bank, World Trade Organisation, European Union, and so on - will continue to limit our freedom to shape our future as we think right. Many of us also feel a sense of interdependence and mutuality with people in other less privileged parts of the world, and a responsibility to help to reform global structures of power for their sake as well as our own.

One thing that many of us share with Attwood, however, is an awareness that the money system needs to be brought up to date. For over two centuries political democracy has been spreading through the world, thanks to Attwood and others like him. But our capacity to control the power of money and harness it to the public good has lagged far behind. So much so that failure to bring the workings of money and finance into line with economic justice and the realities of the Information Age is already damaging confidence in political democracy itself.

We need to bring the corporate power of multinational money under democratic control. That will have to be done within a new framework of:

- global public revenue raising, including taxation,
- global public spending, eg. on United Nations' activities, and
- a global currency, evolving from something like the IMF's Special Drawing Rights (SDRs). [8]

This new global framework will have to be supervised much more effectively at supranational level than international monetary and financial institutions are today. It can then serve the needs of the world's peoples much more fairly and efficiently. An international monetary system, which is based on one or two superpower currencies such as the US$ and (as some people hope) the euro, profits the countries that issue those currencies at the expense of the rest of the world.

For us in Britain the euro highlights the link between democracy and the money system. In spite of efforts to persuade us that scrapping the pound and replacing it with the euro would be a progressive step, people are increasingly doubtful. Why can't we

---

[8] See *Sharing Limited Resources: The Role of Money and Finance: Changing A Central Part of the Problem into a Central Part of the Solution,* James Robertson's paper at the annual conference of the Pio Manzu International Research Centre, Rimini, Italy, October 2003 – www.piomanzu.com.

use the euro as a parallel currency, alongside the pound, rather than a single currency managed by a remote, centralised monetary authority imposing one-size-fits-all interest rates and money supply on millions of diverse people and places? Surely 21st-century pressures to become more globalised *and* more localised call for a more pluralistic monetary system, allowing different currencies and means of payment to evolve at local to global levels, enabling people and organisations to choose to use whichever currency they find most convenient and useful for different purposes. [9]

So - as well as national currencies, continental currencies and a global currency - we should be encouraging currencies issued by local government authorities for local circulation, and non-official payment systems set up by local community groups (like LETSystems), local social service groups (like Time Banks), and local business groups (like the WIR co-operative in Switzerland). In technical terms, whereas paper money could have been accepted as the new basis for the monetary system in Attwood's time, electronic money can now make it convenient for us to use different currencies for different purposes.

That technical factor also points the way to monetary reform at the national level. Dematerialised non-cash money (i.e. electronic bank-created money held in bank accounts and transmitted between them by modern information and telecommunication technology) is now overwhelmingly important. About 97% of this country's money supply is created in that form by commercial banks, and only 3% as banknotes and coins issued by the Bank of England and the Royal Mint. The commercial banks create the non-cash money out of thin air, calling it credit and writing it into their customers' current accounts as profit-making loans. That gives them over £20 billion a year in interest, while the taxpayer gets less than £3 billion a year from the issue of banknotes and coins. Stopping commercial banks creating non-cash money, and transferring to the central bank responsibility for creating it and

---

[9] James Robertson, *Forward with the euro AND the pound*, Economic Research Council, London, 2002.

issuing it debt-free to the government to spend into circulation, will result in extra public revenue of about £45 billion a year. This is the reform with which this book is specifically concerned.[10]

It will mean that:-

1) Taxation and government debt can be reduced, or public spending can be increased, by up to £45 billion a year.

2) The value of a common resource - the national money supply - will become a source of public revenue rather than private profit. That will remove an economic injustice.

3) Withdrawing the present hidden subsidy to the banks will result in a freer market for money and finance, and a more competitive banking industry.

4) A debt-free money supply will help to reduce present levels of public and private debt, which are partly caused by the fact that nearly all the money we use has been created as debt.

5) The economy will become more stable. Banks inevitably want to lend and their customers want to borrow more at the peaks of the business cycle and less in the troughs. So, when the amount of money in circulation depends on how much the banks are lending, the peaks and troughs - the booms and busts - are automatically amplified.

6) The central bank will be better able to control inflation if it itself decides and directly creates the quantity of new money the economy needs. It now tries to control inflation indirectly, by raising interest rates (i.e. the price at which people borrow from banks). But raising costs in that way actually helps to cause inflation. That partly explains why inflation has to be allowed to rise steadily every year – by 2.5% in the UK – in order to avoid deflating the economy.

---

[10] This reform is described by Joseph Huber and James Robertson, *Creating New Money: A monetary reform for the information age*, New Economics Foundation, London, 2000.

7) Environmental stress will be reduced. When, as now, almost all the money we use is debt, people have to produce and sell more things in order to service and repay debt than they would if money were put into circulation debt-free.

In our proposals for this reform, Joseph Huber and I called it "seigniorage reform". Seigniorage was the profit made by monarchs and local rulers from minting and issuing coins. In democratic societies in the Information Age, the proposed reform will restore the prerogative of the state - now on behalf of the people - to capture as public revenue the value of putting the money supply into circulation.

Lessons from Early 19th-Century Britain

The success of the 1832 Reform Bill campaign was due to the coming together of people with different goals, such as repealing the Corn Laws and disconnecting money from gold, because they all saw parliamentary reform as a necessary step towards those goals. Today we are seeing coalitions of progressive non-governmental-organisations (NGOs) with different primary aims - for more democracy, renewable energy, sustainable agriculture, more local production for local consumption, and so on – beginning to promote those aims, not just as separate reforms, but as parts of an integrated reform programme, in which monetary and financial reforms will play a key part.

A group which presented an "Earth Emergency Call To Action" to the Johannesburg World Summit in August 2002 is an example. Their Call To Action demanded the following changes: [11]

---

[11] This declaration was initiated by people from the Schumacher Society, the Sustainable Society, Positive News, the Gaia Foundation and the Right Livelihood Foundation. See *Positive News*, Special Issue , August 2002. It was one of a number of similar civil-society statements published for the Johannesburg Summit. Among the ways it is being followed up is preparatory work to set up a World Future Council – also see Chapter 3, note 35.

- *replace polluting energy systems* in industry, agriculture, transport and the built environment with *renewable energy technology*,

- *co-operate globally to revive local democracies and local economies* - with emphasis on local production for local consumption and less long-distance transport of goods,

- *make sustainable agriculture the global norm* - securing food supplies with minimal environmental impacts,

- create a *participative earth democracy* - fundamentally reforming global governance for the benefit of people and nature, so that international decision making is open and accountable within the framework of a strengthened and democratised United Nations,

- initiate a progressive *shift of funds from military spending towards environmental security* - providing adequate water, nutrition, healthcare, shelter and sustainable livelihoods for all,

- *shift taxation from labour to the use of resources, and pollution and waste* - promoting conservation and clean production, and enhancing social welfare and jobs, and

- *reform worldwide monetary and financial systems* to protect and enhance the well-being of human communities and the natural environment on which they depend.

These last three points clearly indicate that monetary and financial reform is going to play a much more central part in today's campaigns for wider political and economic change than it did in the past. Many more people now understand that money is power, and that the institutions of money today negate democracy by using their power to exploit people and keep them dependent. Many more people also understand that money is a scoring system - for the game of economic life - and that the way this scoring system works today is systematically perverse: it rewards undesirable activities, penalises desirable ones, and frustrates desirable change in almost every sphere.

In short, campaigners for change in many fields are increasingly coming to see monetary and financial reform as vital to the achievement of their particular aims, just as their predecessors in Thomas Attwood's time saw parliamentary reform as vital to the achievement of theirs. The particular proposal for monetary reform we are discussing in this book is a key part of that.

CHAPTER 2

MONETARY REFORM TODAY
and some Obstacles and Objections to it
By James Robertson

The Proposed Reform

The particular reform we are discussing concerns public currencies. These include the pound, the dollar and the yen that belong to nations, and the euro that belongs to a group of nations. In future they will include a genuine world currency that does not yet exist.

National governments are responsible for seeing that national currencies maintain their value and provide an essential public service to the population as a whole. In that respect these currencies differ from the more private kinds of currencies and quasi-currencies used by community groups (like LETS) or groups of businesses (like the Swiss club WIR) for transactions between their members, and loyalty points, Air Miles, etc issued by companies to customers or suppliers, who may then use them as a means of exchange.

In the more pluralistic multi-level-currency era foreseen in Chapter 1, the principles of the proposed national currency reform will apply to other official currencies. These will include local currencies to meet the need of local communities within their particular localities, and a global currency to meet the need of the world community for a means of transnational exchange. One of the principles is that the profit (or 'seigniorage') arising from creating money of this kind should be public revenue, not private profit. Another is that these public currencies should be created debt-free, not as interest-bearing repayable debt. We will return shortly to the implications of this for international monetary reform.

Meanwhile, to recapitulate from Chapter 1, the proposed national monetary reform is as follows:

1)   As national monetary authorities, central banks should create non-cash money (i.e. bank-account money) as well as cash (i.e. banknotes and coins). They should create out of thin air at regular intervals the amounts they decide are needed to increase the money supply. They should give these amounts to their governments as debt-free public revenue. Governments should then put the money into circulation by spending it.

2)   It should become illegal for anyone else to create bank-account money denominated in the national currency, just as it is already illegal to forge coins or counterfeit banknotes.

This will involve the following changes:

1)   The central bank will no longer regulate increases in the money supply by manipulating the interest rates at which commercial banks lend into circulation money they create for that purpose. The central bank will be directly responsible for deciding how much is needed and for creating it and issuing it itself.

2)   Commercial banks will be prohibited from creating money. They will have to borrow already existing money in order to lend it, as other financial intermediaries do.

This will parallel what happened with banknotes in 19th-century England (see Chapter 1). Electronic bank-deposit money has now become real money and it is time to stop pretending it is just credit. As the issue of banknotes became subject to seigniorage then, so the creation of bank-account money should become subject to it now. In other words, the profit from creating it should no longer accrue to commercial banks but be collected as public revenue. The best available estimate is that in Britain this would contribute about £45bn a year to public revenue, and deprive commercial banks of the 'subsidy' - estimated at over £20bn a year - which they now get from interest on the new money they are allowed to create.

The beneficial economic and social effects of this reform have been summarised in Chapter 1 (pp20-21). They are very great. Moreover, the reform would be evolutionary, not revolutionary. Since the Second World War the Bank of England has continued to evolve from being a commercial bank with a special relationship to the government, towards becoming a straightforward agency of the state as its central monetary authority. At the same time, the commercial banks have continued to evolve towards being free-market businesses, with fewer public service obligations backed by government subsidies and controls. For both the Bank of England and the commercial banks, the proposed reform is the next step in that process of evolution.

Seigniorage and the Global Economy

Whoever creates new money can either give it away or benefit from putting it into circulation by spending it or lending it at interest. Just as, under the proposed national reform, the benefit from creating national-currency money would go to the national community as a whole, a comparable change at the international level would benefit the world community as a whole. It would replace the present use of the US dollar and other national currencies like the yen, the euro and the pound as 'reserve currencies', by a world currency issued by a world monetary authority, and channel the profit from issuing it into public revenue to be spent on behalf of the world community. This global reform would clearly need simultaneous support from many national governments. That does not necessarily mean that one country could not undertake national monetary reform on its own. But it would clearly be easier for single nations to do it, if the global version of the same reform was on the global agenda.

In 1995 the independent international Commission on Global Governance[12] identified the United States' "unique luxury of being able to borrow in its own currency abroad and then devalue its repayment obligations" as one of the weaknesses of the current international monetary system. It pointed out that "a growing world economy requires constant enlargement of international liquidity", and suggested that issue of the IMF's reserve currency - Special Drawing Rights (SDRs) - should be increased.

In 2000 in *Creating New Money*[13] we suggested that SDRs might develop into a global currency which would eventually replace the US dollar and other national currencies in that role. Following the model we had proposed for national seigniorage reform, we suggested this global money might be issued - perhaps by a new international agency combining some of the functions of the IMF and the Bank for International Settlements - into an operational account which it would hold for the United Nations. The UN would spend this money into circulation, partly as a contribution to financing its own operations, and perhaps partly by distributing it to national governments according to the size of their populations.

This new international agency, which would in due course come to be seen as an embryonic world central bank, would have to combine accountability with a high degree of independence in its decisions about how much new international money to create. It might agree the broad terms of its mission with a UN policy-making body accountable to member governments, as a published framework within which to carry out its responsibility for global monetary policy. It might report and be accountable for its performance either to that UN body or to another, such as a committee of the General Assembly.

---

[12] Commission on Global Governance, *Our Global Neighbourhood*, Oxford University Press, 1995: pp 180-188.
[13] op cit, Chapter 5.10, pp 57-58.   /

In the past three years the significance of the 'dollar hegemony' of the United States, and the urgent need for international monetary reform, have become more widely understood.

For example, one report calculates that every American citizen owes the rest of the world $7,333, while every citizen of the developing countries owes it only $500. But, while developing country economies must pay debt service repayments totalling more than $300bn a year, the US must only pay $20bn a year to service an almost equivalent amount of debt. Americans have been engaged in a consumer binge, which has led to the largest current account deficit in history, a staggering $445 billion or 4% of US GDP. This deficit has been increasing by 50% a year in recent years, and economists predict it will rise to $730bn by 2006. Given this daily deficit of up to £2bn, plus capital outflow of $2bn, the US in effect has to borrow $4bn from the pool of world savings every day. More disturbingly, it is being financed by the poor through capital flight from poor countries and the forced holdings of high levels of dollar reserves. To build up reserves, poor countries have to borrow hard currency from the US at interest rates as high as 18%; and lend it back to the US in the form of Treasury Bonds at 3% interest.[14]

Another report finds that "ever since 1971, when US president Richard Nixon took the dollar off the gold standard, the dollar has been a global monetary instrument that the United States, and only the United States, can produce by fiat. ... World trade is now a game in which the US produces dollars and the rest of the world produces things that dollars can buy. The world's interlinked economies compete in exports to capture needed dollars to service dollar-denominated foreign debts and to accumulate dollar reserves ".[15]

---

[14] Romilly Greenhill and Ann Pettifor, *The United States as a HIPC (heavily indebted prosperous country) - how the poor are financing the rich*, New Economics Foundation, London, 2002; www.neweconomics.org
[15] Henry C K Liu, *US Dollar Hegemony Has Got To Go,* Asia Times Online Co Ltd, 2002.

A third example: "At the root of this new form of imperialism is the exploitation of governments by a single government, that of the United States via the central banks and multilateral control institutions of intergovernmental capital... What has turned the older form of imperialism into a super imperialism is that, whereas prior to the 1960s the US government dominated international organisation by virtue of its preeminent creditor status, since that time it has done so by virtue of its debtor position".[16]

Finally, the researches of Richard Douthwaite and the Irish NGO Feasta[17] confirm that the total annual subsidy (or 'tribute') received by the US from the rest of the world as a result of dollar seigniorage is at least $400bn a year. This is roughly comparable to the annual US balance of payments deficit. It also explains how the US has been able to maintain its extraordinary scale of annual military expenditure compared with all other countries. The huge dollar seigniorage subsidy has even been justified by some US commentators as a payment by the rest of the world to the US as the 'policeman' on whom the world relies to keep order! However, as Douthwaite notes, "given the policeman's record of destabilising or overthrowing governments with which he has had ideological differences and the fact that he would continue to put his 'particularistic national interests' ahead of those of the rest of the world, I doubt if many countries would be entirely happy with the arrangement".

---

[16] Michael Hudson, *Super Imperialism: The Origin and Fundamentals of World Domination*, Pluto Press, 2003, pp23-24.

[17] Richard Douthwaite, *Defense and the Dollar*, 2002 and Feasta, *Climate and Currency: Proposals for Global Monetary Reform*, 2002, prepared for the Johannesburg World Summit on Sustainable Development. Details of both from The Foundation for the Economics of Sustainability, 9 Lower Rathmines Road, Dublin 6, Republic of Ireland; e-mail: feasta@anu.ie; web: www.feasta.org

These analyses show up not only the injustice of the present way of creating money for international and global purposes, but also suggest how distorting and damaging it is to global economic efficiency and financial stability. They clearly point to the need for international monetary reform on a similar basis to the proposed national reform - involving the creation of international money debt-free by an agency which serves the interests of the world community as a whole and provides seigniorage revenue to be spent on global public purposes. As international campaigning grows stronger for international reform on those lines it will reinforce the pressure for comparable national reforms.

Dealing with Obstacles and Objections

The following are among the obstacles to national monetary reform and the objections put forward against it:

1) powerful opposition from banking and financial interests (and from associated constituencies of professionals, academics and politicians), and threats that even the prospect of monetary reform would destabilise the economy;

2) public ignorance and confusion about the present arrangements;

3) an elitist belief that ignorance about them is positively desirable;

4) ignorance and obfuscation about what the monetary reform proposals actually are;

5) the claim that they would involve a further centralisation of state power;

6) the assumption that the reform would be inflationary;

7) the assumption that it would 'crowd out' investment in the private sector;

8) the argument that depriving banks of the present seigniorage subsidy would increase the costs of borrowing, would raise the costs of payment services, and would force banks to cut costs, close branches and reduce jobs;

9) the argument that it would damage the international competitiveness of British banks and therefore of the British economy as a whole;

10) the argument that no other country has undertaken, or is seriously considering, this reform.

So how are these obstacles and objections to be dealt with? And how far will they have to be dealt with internationally?

Obstacle/Objection 1.
Opposition from powerful banking and financial interests and the threat of economic destabilisation.

This obstacle will be overcome only when the arguments for monetary reform are more widely understood, when opposition to it is more widely recognised as mere defence of private privilege, and when its opponents accept that they risk losing more by continuing to oppose it than by losing the present subsidy. National and international advocacy and campaigning will be needed to bring that situation about.

Obstacle/Objection 2.
Ignorance and confusion about how new money is now created.

Many people, even in government and parliament, don't know how new money is now created, and what the consequences are. Most people find it hard to believe, if they think about it at all, that almost all the money in circulation has been created by commercial banks at profit to themselves. In reply to questions, a government spokesman may say that the funds which banks lend to customers "must either be obtained from depositors or the sterling money market, both of which usually require the payment of interest" - thus appearing to deny that banks are allowed to create new money and to profit from doing so.[18] Simon Hughes MP wrote to a constituent on 20 November 2001 that "banks don't

---

[18] Written answer to Lord Beaumont of Whitley, House of Lords, 23 November 2000.

print money but create credit".[19] More often, however, the government accepts that banks create money and defends this by saying that "if banks were obliged to bid for funds from lenders in order to make loans to their customers, the costs to banks of extending credit would rise significantly." [20] Two recent parliamentary Early Day Motions - EDM 1515 on "Using The Public Credit" by Austin Mitchell MP on 26 June 2002 and EDM 854 on "Publicly Created Money And Monetary Reform" by David Chaytor MP on 10 March 2003,[21] indicate a growing parliamentary awareness of the facts – an awareness which David Boyle on "The Strange Rebirth of a Forgotten Idea" (*New Statesman*, 7 April 2003) helped to spread more widely. People who are in any doubt about how money is created might glance at Chapter 22-3 of a current 'students' bible' on economics.[22] It explains "how banks create money" and that "bank-created deposit money is much the largest part of the money supply in modern economies".

The action needed is to press Treasury Ministers and the Bank of England to clarify and publicise

- how almost all new money is now created,
- who benefits and who suffers thereby, and
- whether or not the estimates of an annual hidden subsidy of more than £20bn to the banks, and a failure to collect more than £40bn potential public revenue, are broadly correct.

This action need not be international to make some impact. But, if individuals and NGOs in other countries were to press the same demand on their finance ministries and central banks, the impact would be greater.

---

[19] I am grateful to Canon Peter Challen for this information.
[20] Letter to Archie Norman MP from Treasury Minister Melanie Johnson, 18 October 2000. I am grateful to Brian Leslie for this information.
[21] Further information will be found via http://edm.ais.co.uk. Otherwise ask House of Commons Information Office – Tel. +44 (0)20 7219 4272.
[22] David Begg, Stanley Fischer and Rudiger Dornbusch, *Economics*, McGraw-Hill, 7th edition, 2003, pp 316 and 318.

Obstacle/Objection 3.
The view that ignorance and confusion are positively desirable.

It has been suggested that the deflationary crisis in Japan may have reached a depth which requires the government explicitly to create new money. But when a member of the British economic elite wrote publicly on those lines last year, he felt it necessary to accompany it with a warning that that policy should be avoided in Europe if possible, because "ideally we should avoid unconventional approaches. For the conventions of central bank independence, and of non-transparent money creation, are based on well founded fears that governments will abuse direct control of money printing presses". [23]

The specific argument that monetary reform would open the way to uncontrollable inflation is dealt with later. Here we have to overcome the more general argument that the present "non-transparent" system of money creation should be maintained; in other words, that citizens and politicians of democratic countries should be kept in the dark about how money is now created and how the present system might be reformed.

Again, this points to the need to press the authorities to explain how almost all new money is now created, what are the arguments for and against creating it that way, and how much the present system benefits the commercial banks and reduces potential public revenue. The pressure need not be international in order to make an impact on national thinking, but the impact would be greater if it were.

---

[23] Adair Turner, *Europe's Best Defence Against Deflation,* Financial Times, 4 November 2002.

Obstacle/Objection 4.
Ignorance and confusion about the actual reform proposal.

The proposed reform would not entail, as a House of Commons Library researcher wrongly advised Robert Jackson MP in March 2001,[24] that the central bank should be given responsibility and power to decide how new money shall be used, so making it responsible for fiscal policy as well as monetary policy and depriving the elected government of power to manage the economy! The central bank will merely decide what increases are needed in the money supply, create them, and give them to the government as public revenue, leaving the elected government to decide - as with taxes and other public revenue - how the money is to be used. At present, of course, it is the commercial banks who decide *both* how much new money to create *and* who shall borrow it for what purposes.

Those who propagate this error must be publicly corrected. International support, though helpful, will not be strictly necessary for that.

Obstacle/Objection 5.
Opposition to supposed increased centralisation of state power.

Linked with the misunderstanding at 4 above is the claim that the reform will increase the centralised power of the state. Opposition to reform on this ground comes from two rather different quarters.

On the one hand there are members of the mainstream economic and political elite who are happy with the present situation in Britain, with the Big Four multinational banks sharing a virtual monopoly of money creation under the Bank of England's central control of interest rates. Michael Portillo MP is one. A response to his view is under Obstacle/Objection 9 below.

---

[24] I am grateful to Mr Jackson for letting me see this advice.

On the other hand, there are decentralist monetary reformers who champion the emergence and spread of alternative currency schemes to serve localities, communities, and groups of businesses, and what is sometimes called 'free banking'. Some decentralists, like David Boyle, doubt "whether it is possible or desirable in the modern day to give the state a monopoly of official currency".[25]

If it is unacceptably centralising to treat new national money as a public resource, to collect its value as public revenue, and to distribute it via public spending programmes, the same principle should presumably apply to the state's monopoly of national taxation and public spending. Imagine for a moment that the history of taxation and public spending had led to them being managed now on a profit-making basis by the Big Four banks. Would decentralists be responding to proposals for reform with the objection that it isn't "possible or desirable to give the state a monopoly of national taxation and public spending"?

Actually there is no contradiction between mainstream monetary reform and decentralised monetary innovation. Both embody the principle that money should serve the needs of people (not vice versa). If you accept that plural currencies are likely to serve people's needs better than a single one-size-fits-all currency for all purposes, both are desirable. There is no reason why support for alternative currencies should mean continuing to accept the present mainstream arrangements, except a wholly unrealistic hope that the new alternative, community, and other private currencies will grow rapidly enough to replace the mainstream system within the foreseeable future.

The practical fact is that in a democratic society, unlike other forms of society, additions to the money supply put into circulation as public revenue will tend to be distributed just as wisely and fairly, if not more so, via increases in public spending

---

[25] David Boyle, *The Money Changers: currency reform from Aristotle to e-cash*, Earthscan, London, 2002, p134.

and reductions in taxes and public debt than the new money now created by the commercial banks as loans to their customers.

To sum up, there should be no sense of conflict between decentralist and mainstream monetary reformers. Both should work together nationally and internationally to spread wider understanding that radical monetary change is urgent and that their approaches are both necessary.

Obstacle/Objection 6.
Monetary reform will be inflationary.

People have learned from history that allowing governments to create new money is a recipe for inflation. So a conventional knee-jerk response to the proposed monetary reform is that it will be inflationary.

It is true that money creation by feudal and monarchical governments in the past and by elected governments more recently has led to inflation. But that does not mean inflation will result from giving an operationally independent central bank responsibility for creating new money directly, instead of indirectly influencing by interest-rate changes how much the commercial banks create. Many people don't yet realise that in 1997 the conduct of monetary policy in Britain was changed. The Bank of England was restructured as an operationally independent central monetary authority. It is accountable to the Chancellor of the Exchequer and Parliament for achieving the published monetary policy objectives which they have framed and approved. But it now carries out this task free from interference by elected ministers and politicians and their staffs. Monetary reform in those new circumstances will enable the Bank to control inflation more effectively, not less effectively, than at present.

The action required to get this more widely understood does not have to be international. But, if it is, the impact may well be greater.

Obstacle/Objection 7.
The proposed reform would 'crowd out' investment in the private sector.

This is another spurious conventional reaction. It argues that creating new money as government revenue will 'crowd out' investment in the wealth-creating private sector and switch it to the wealth-consuming public sector: "by only allocating resources to the public services, private sector investment would, in effect, be crowded out, implying that the Government knows best when past experience suggests otherwise".[26]

But of course the proposed reform need not result in allocating resources only to the public sector. Governments could equally well use the new source of revenue to cut taxes and the national debt and so stimulate private investment and consumer spending. Even if new money does circulate via public spending, it will soon reach businesses and citizens who can use it for private sector investment or consumption as they themselves decide.

The irony is that both the present Labour government and its Conservative predecessor have committed themselves to large Private Finance Initiative (PFI) schemes. These are specifically designed to divert private sector investment finance into public sector investment projects - at very high public cost. Neither the City nor the government has objected that PFI schemes crowd out genuine private sector investment. Their real objection to monetary reform is about losing the subsidy to private profits provided by the present method of creating new money.

Although action to demolish this particular knee-jerk objection to monetary reform need not be international, an effective international reform campaign could be helpful in this context, as in others.

---

[26] Letter to Dennis Canavan MP from Treasury Minister Melanie Johnson, 6 September 2000. I am grateful to Alan Armstrong for this information.

Obstacle/Objection 8.
Depriving banks of the present seigniorage subsidy would increase the costs of borrowing, raise the costs of payments services, and force banks to cut costs, close branches and reduce jobs.

We have noted earlier the Treasury view that the impact of monetary reform "on the cost of borrowing would be significant, adversely affecting business investment, especially of small and medium-sized firms." [27] In fact, this will not necessarily be true. Nor will it be the whole story.

The banking industry will become more competitive when it is no longer subsidised, and the oligopoly of lending to small businesses now enjoyed by the "Big Four" will be more easily challenged by other banks. That will tend to reduce the costs of borrowing. Furthermore, when money is put into circulation debt-free, the costs of servicing and repaying debt that the use of debt-created money now imposes on every economic transaction will be eliminated, with the result that less borrowing will be needed than now because that element in the present cost of all economic activity will no longer have to be met.

As regards the costs and efficiency of payments services,[28] it is true that if banks are no longer subsidised by the profit they now get from creating money but have to borrow money at interest to lend to their customers, they will no longer be able to cross-subsidise their payments services as much as at present. Initially, costs to bank customers may rise as they have to meet the full costs of the payments services they use.

But, although withdrawing subsidies from any industry initially makes the cost of its products higher, it is generally recognised that this kind of cross-subsidisation between different services is an impediment to competitiveness and economic efficiency.

---

[27] Letter to Archie Norman MP from Treasury Minister Melanie Johnson, 18 October 2000.
[28] This point was touched on by Treasury Minister Ruth Kelly in her letter of 20 August 2001 - see under Obstacle/Objection 9 below.

It is also true that withdrawing the present subsidy will encourage banks to cut costs, perhaps involving further closure of branches and loss of banking jobs. Withdrawing subsidies from any subsidised industry, including coal, steel, ship-building and many others, has had effects of that kind. But subsidies have been withdrawn in the knowledge that subsidies to an industry reduce its competitiveness, by making it more difficult for smaller firms to compete with bigger ones and more difficult for new innovative entrants into the industry to establish themselves. So far as the economy as a whole is concerned, subsidies to particular industries tend to hold back innovation and reduce the growth of efficiency and productivity by distorting the allocation of resources.

Are there any special reasons why the banking and financial services industry should be sheltered from these facts of economic life, except the mystique and power it now exercises over political decision makers? That question calls for research and analysis on a greater scale and a more open-minded basis than has been carried out hitherto. This offers a new field of study for up-and-coming economists.

Campaigning in one country could effectively question whether banking should be treated as a special case in this respect. But international campaigning might have greater impact.

Obstacle/Objection 9.
Depriving banks of the hidden subsidy will weaken their ability to compete internationally with other countries' banks.

This view is a favourite with opponents of reform. It was powerfully expressed in letters to correspondents from Michael Portillo as Shadow Chancellor of the Exchequer (28 September 2000 and 13 February 2001).[29] He said he "would not support proposals that gave the State the monopoly on non-cash money.

---

[29] My thanks to Margaret Harvey, Barbara Panvel, John Bunzl and Jack Hornsby for this information.

Legislating against the credit multiplier would lead to the migration from the City of London of the largest collection of banks in the world. It would be a disaster for the British economy".

Each of Mr. Portillo's statement is questionable. "Giving the state a monopoly of non-cash money" is an exaggerated way of saying that an agency of the state would decide and create the amount of new national money required to meet the objectives of monetary policy, and give it to the government to spend it into circulation, instead of allowing a small group of big commercial banks to create it and put it into circulation as profit-making loans to selected bank customers. See Obstacle/Objections 4 and 5 above for comment on that point. The term "credit multiplier" aims to conceal the fact that new national money is being created for private profit. Whether depriving commercial banks of that privilege would lead to the migration from the City of London of the largest collection of banks in the world, and whether - even if that happened - it would be a disaster for the British economy and society as a whole, are moot points. They need more serious research and analysis, not just knee-jerk assumptions. In fact, it is likely that, after a short period of adaptation by the banking and financial sector, the outcome would prove beneficial to British society as a whole, including the economy's international competitiveness.

Much the same point as Mr. Portillo's was made by Treasury Minister Ruth Kelly in a letter of 20 August 2001 to Robert Jackson MP.[30] She said, "It is evident that this proposal would cause a dramatic loss in profits to the banks - all else equal they would still face the costs of running the payments system but would not be able to make profitable loans using the deposits held in current accounts. In this case it is highly likely that banks will attempt to maintain their profitability by re-locating to avoid the restriction on their operations that the proposed reform involves. Given the desirability of an internationally competitive market in

---

[30] I am grateful to Mr Jackson for sending me a copy.

financial (and other) services, it would not be in the UK's interests to insulate itself from such a market".

But why should monetary reform mean the UK insulating itself from an internationally competitive market for banking and financial services? As has already been suggested, far from being a disaster, withdrawing the banks' present subsidy might prove beneficial to their competitiveness and certainly to the competitiveness of the economy as a whole.

The subject needs much more serious analysis and research than it has yet had. That does not need to be carried out in more than one country to be valid. But we must remember, as Machiavelli pointed out in 1532 in *The Prince*, that "he who introduces a new order of things has all those who profit from the old order as his enemies, and he has only lukewarm allies in all those who might profit from the new". However valid the arguments and the research supporting it may turn out to be, it may be difficult to persuade politicians and the public that, in the context of international competition, the risks attaching to monetary reform by one country alone are worth taking. At all events, an international programme of analysis, research and campaigning will be very desirable.

Obstacle/Objection 10.
No other country is seriously considering monetary reform.

In a letter of 1st November 2001 Treasury Minister Ruth Kelly wrote to Robert Jackson MP, "To the best of my knowledge, no support amongst developed countries or international economic institutions exists" for monetary reform.[31] This brings to mind the joke about the economist who tells his grandson not to bother picking up a £5 note from the pavement, because if it were real somebody else would have picked it up already!

There will probably be no harm, and much gain, in being first to introduce monetary reform, if it will make the economy as a

---

[31] Again, I am grateful to Mr Jackson for letting me see this.

whole more efficient and productive, and society more just and inclusive. However, the special interests of the banking industry are likely to find support from politicians and individuals who feel that the risks of being a pioneer outweigh the possible rewards.

So once again, international efforts to promote monetary reform will clearly be important.

Summing up therefore, it seems clear that, although there is still a great deal of progress to be made within one country such as Britain to mobilise an effective campaign for monetary reform, international research, analysis, advocacy and campaigning will also play a key part. Whether or not monetary reform in one country must depend on monetary reform in others is a different question. We now turn to it.

CHAPTER 3

THE SIMULTANEOUS POLICY APPROACH
By John Bunzl

Introduction

As the preceding chapter indicates, in today's increasingly globalised and interconnected world, reforms which could once have been implemented on a unilateral national basis without further ado now need to be considered much more carefully by policy makers. This is because the implications and effects of new policy are likely to reach far beyond national borders and beyond the sector of the economy they directly concern. Governments must now assess virtually all important potential policy changes with a view to how they will affect the competitiveness of their industries and services against those of other countries and how capital markets are likely to react to such changes.

Today's capital markets operate globally and developing countries are encouraged to follow the richer countries by opening up their economies and financial markets to global flows of goods, services and capital. Corporations generally move or subcontract their manufacturing operations to any part of the world where labour or environmental costs are lowest and profits therefore highest. Financial markets also switch capital investments at short notice from one economy to another depending on the prospects each country offers for profitable gain. In a globalised world, the sensitivity of national governments to these movements means that governance is today no longer a domestically isolated, "absolute" affair but has become, rather, a highly *relative* one. The success or failure of government policy is today largely determined not solely by national domestic factors but increasingly by its relative effects on international markets as compared to the policies of other competing nations.

Furthermore, the instantaneous nature of global information and financial networks and the short-term profit orientation of financial markets forces governments and politicians to be even more wary of implementing any reform which might be perceived as unwelcome by global markets. The unilateral implementation of such reforms could risk an adverse market reaction and a consequent negative impact on that nation's economy, even if that impact might only be adverse for a short period. This far more complicated, volatile and risky environment not only makes it difficult for governments to adopt controversial or untried policies such as Monetary Reform, it equally provides an "excuse-rich environment" which allows politicians to justify not doing so. While some academics dispute the severity of the influence of global markets on the policy-making options of advanced democracies such as the USA and the EU, there seems to be little argument about the fact that there *is* such an influence and that it is relatively strong.[32] There is also substantial agreement that market influence on economically weaker developing countries is very strong indeed allowing their governments very little, if any, room for manoeuvre.

In short, there is little doubt that important unilateral changes to national policy have generally become much more difficult in a globalised world. Governments now seem to be paralysed within a straitjacket of narrow, market-friendly policy parameters which permit only incremental and inadequate change just at a time when global challenges such as global warming, monopolist corporate power, international terrorism, mounting debt and global poverty demand urgent and decisive action. Since the policies required to solve these problems, such as much tighter environmental standards, tighter regulations on corporations and financial markets and so on, are generally unattractive to global investors, the problems remain inadequately addressed and are

---

[32] See for example, *Global Capital and National Governments,* Layna Mosley, Cambridge University Press, 2003.

consequently allowed to worsen further. Crucially, this policy straitjacket also means that, once they reach office, political parties of whatever colour are forced to conform broadly to this narrow policy framework regardless of their pre-election manifesto promises or of the views of the electorate. This situation fundamentally undermines the principles of democracy since, to an increasing extent, policies favoured by global investors take precedence over those desired by electorates.

It is against the background of this dilemma that we consider the Simultaneous Policy (SP) concept - and the campaign which has grown from it - as a means for overcoming the obstacles and objections to Monetary Reform raised in the preceding chapter. It should also be borne in mind, however, that these objections are likely to apply also to many other economic, environmental and social reforms called for by activist groups and NGOs which constitute the global justice movement.[33]

What is the Simultaneous Policy and what are the aims of the International Simultaneous Policy Organisation (ISPO)?

The Simultaneous Policy (SP) campaign was launched in 2000.[34] ISPO is a growing association of citizens world-wide who are gradually organising in many countries to use their votes in a new, co-ordinated and effective way to drive all nations to cooperate in solving the many global problems the world is now confronted with. ISPO's members recognise that these problems cannot be solved while governments are forced to operate within an effective policy straitjacket dictated by global markets. Only by ushering in a fundamentally cooperative world order by which citizens bring their democratically elected governments to reassert

---

[33] The term, *'global justice movement',* is used to describe all manner of non-governmental organisations, activist organisations and campaigning groups and individual citizens who are working for social, environmental or political reform, locally, nationally or globally.

[34] For a full explanation of the campaign, see: *The Simultaneous Policy – An Insider's Guide to saving Humanity and the Planet,* by John Bunzl. New European Publications, 2001.

proper authority over global markets can the nations of the world work together to find and implement solutions. ISPO's citizen members around the world seek to overcome the present governmental paralysis by gradually bringing all nations to adopt in principle - and then to simultaneously implement - the Simultaneous Policy (SP), a range of policy measures to bring about economic justice, environmental security and peace around the world.

To properly comprehend the SP proposal, the reader should note that a fundamental distinction must be made between the *adoption* of SP – i.e. its adoption in principle – and its *implementation*. Citizens, politicians and political parties will be encouraged to *adopt* SP but it is only to be *implemented* when all – or sufficient – nations do likewise. Adoption of SP is therefore a gradual process, whereas its implementation would occur simultaneously only when all, or sufficient, nations had first adopted it.

The policy measures SP is to consist of will ultimately be designed (or consented to) by ISPO's citizen members who may, if they wish, delegate the task of formulating those measures to an expert and independent group of alternative policy makers.[35] The measures of SP could therefore include *Creating New Money* or similar proposals as well as a synthesis of all the many other reforms called for by the global justice movement. It should be noted, therefore, that SP is a policy that *ISPO's citizen members themselves* will decide upon and determine – *not* one that is dictated by politicians, political parties, business or by global institutions such as the WTO.[36] A further key point to note is that the condition of *simultaneous* implementation by all nations removes each nation's fear of losing out to others; it effectively removes the key objection of first-mover disadvantage. The policy

---

[35] Possible candidates for such a role could include the proposed World Future Council (see Chapter 1, note 11) or the Club of Budapest or some other group of independent and internationally respected policy experts.

[36] It should be pointed out that the policy measures of SP remain to be developed and defined. It is therefore NOT a policy 'cast in stone', but rather a 'policy-in-the-making'; a policy that is to be developed by ISPO members as the SP campaign develops.

content of SP could thus include all and any desirable policy which hitherto could not be contemplated for fear that unilateral implementation might impair a nation's economic competitiveness or attractiveness to global markets.

But beyond being merely a collection of policy measures, SP is also a *political process*; a process by which its policy measures can come to be implemented.

This is because, rather than merely choosing between the largely indistinguishable policies offered by the existing political parties, as voters conventionally do today, ISPO instead offers citizens world-wide the opportunity of turning the tables on politicians by instead pledging to vote in future elections for <u>ANY</u> personally acceptable political party or candidate that adopts SP. By having their own policy, ISPO's members remove the policy monopoly hitherto possessed by the political parties and, by pledging to vote for ANY party within reason that adopts SP, they also force the political parties to compete fiercely with one another to adopt it.

In an environment where more and more parliamentary seats around the world – and even entire elections – are being won or lost on very small margins, and with voter apathy on the rise, this new way for citizens to use their votes is expected to be capable of presenting politicians in all countries with an attractive, yet compelling, "carrot and stick" proposition. Since SP is only to be implemented simultaneously, there's absolutely no political risk to politicians who adopt it. Indeed, this crucially means that politicians and governments can adopt SP while continuing to pursue policies which safeguard their nation's economic competitiveness until such time as all or sufficient nations have also adopted it. But failing to adopt SP could cost them dearly, especially if they're fighting closely contested elections, for they'll be in severe danger of losing to rivals who *have* adopted SP to attract the SP voting bloc. So SP's growing number of citizen adopters – even if relatively few - could make the vital difference between politicians winning or losing their seats, or even an entire election. As such, the SP process potentially offers a means by which citizens and NGOs, via their adoption of SP, can apply *real electoral pressure* on politicians, rather than relying merely on the more traditional methods of lobbying, consumer boycotts or street protest, important though these are. It should also be noted that this novel way for citizens to use their votes is likely to appeal strongly to the world's fastest-growing political constituency: the apathetic/protest voter.[37]

This new type of electoral pressure could also be particularly important when it comes to ensuring that the USA cooperates with SP. For as we saw in the previous chapter, the USA presently benefits enormously from the dollar's use as the world's main reserve currency with most commodities and loans being dollar-denominated. We should not therefore expect that the 'tribute' exacted by the U.S. from other countries, and estimated to be approximately $400bn per year, would be willingly given up. Therefore, as an example of how SP could potentially be used by American citizens to ensure U.S. cooperation with SP, the following scenario should help to explain:

It will be recalled that in the U.S. Presidential election held in 2000, support for the two main parties was very finely balanced with the Republicans prevailing over the Democrats by only about 2000 votes in Florida. Now, if one were to imagine that by the time of a future Presidential election, the National U.S. Simultaneous Policy Organisation (Simpol-USA) had been able to secure the adoption of SP by, say, 5000 people in Florida and by a similar critical number in the other key US states, then assuming a similar situation as in 2000, both major parties would likely find themselves under extreme pressure to adopt SP. This is because Simpol-USA would, with the agreement of its adopter members, have publicly announced the number of adopters it had in each State and would have openly confirmed that all SP adopters

---

[37] As one ISPO member, Mark Davey, commented: "In the twenty years that I have been afforded a vote, I am unashamed to say that I have never used it. My theory was that not to vote was the best way of securing my protest to all or any political parties. As the years have gone on, my decision at 18 to adopt this tactic has been fuelled by what is happening in the world. As soon as I had digested [the Simultaneous Policy], I signed up to it without hesitation and now feel almost compelled to get involved. Congratulations!"

would be voting for *which ever of the two candidates adopted SP first.*

In such circumstances, if the sitting President failed to adopt SP, s/he would likely lose the Presidency for the simple reason that his/her opponent would likely have adopted SP to attract the all-important crucial extra votes represented by the SP voting bloc. At the same time, however, both contenders would know that neither risks anything politically or economically by adopting SP because implementation only occurs when all or sufficient nations do likewise. In such a scenario, even the influence of heavy corporate funding for either or both candidates would be unlikely to deter either candidate from adopting because the need of each to attract the SP voting bloc would have become paramount and absolutely essential to their political self-interests. For that reason it is quite likely that *both* candidates would have adopted SP: the ideal outcome!

So although no one underestimates the practical difficulties in arriving at such a scenario, our point is that, through SP, US citizens in cooperation with other citizen adopters of SP around the world, have the potential to ensure that even the most dominant nation in the world can, if need be, be brought to cooperate. And the numbers needed to do so could, relatively speaking, be quite small.

At the time of writing, the SP campaign is already underway on an informal basis in a number of countries around the world. It is envisaged that, as the number of SP adopters in each country reaches a significant level, National SP Organisations (NSPOs) will gradually be formed and the first of these is likely to be in the UK. The incorporation of Simpol-UK is scheduled to occur during 2004 as a non-profit company limited by guarantee with all UK members having a vote in its management. It is anticipated that NSPOs will also shortly be formed in Canada, the USA and Australia where the number of adopters is also approaching a viable level.

It is envisaged that the SP adoption campaign would be taken forward in each country by local SP campaign groups, each based on a parliamentary/congressional constituency area. At the time of writing, some local SP groups are already in existence. Their purpose is to campaign for the adoption of SP in their respective constituency or electoral area, aiming to gain as many adoptions from individual citizens as possible with a view to reaching the critical number needed for it to be in the electoral interests of established political party candidates to adopt SP. As that critical number is reached in a constituency, existing party candidates are likely to feel a need to adopt SP either in a bid to gain the additional votes needed to win the parliamentary seat or, in the case of a sitting MP, to avoid losing it. Given this overall plan, it would be perfectly possible for more than one candidate, or even for *all* candidates, to adopt SP. Clearly, the more candidates that do, the better. It is also to be expected that each NSPO would, in the first instance, focus its campaigning priorities on marginal constituencies where adoption by candidates is likely to be achieved most easily, thus providing encouragement to the campaigns in other constituencies and countries.

It will be noted that the above strategy is primarily appropriate to non-proportional, "first-past-the-post" electoral systems such as those that exist in the UK or the USA. However, since electoral systems vary from country to country, ISPO has already developed modified strategies for countries with proportional representation (PR) systems. In addition, a global ISPO coordinating body is also likely to be required to support the activities of all NSPOs as they gradually come into existence and at the time of writing such an organisation is in the planning stages. It is therefore envisaged that, as more and more citizens around the world adopt SP, a 'local to global' organisational structure will evolve to serve both of ISPO's key objectives. Those being, on the one hand to secure sufficient adoptions of SP by citizens, political parties and nations and, on the other, to build an infrastructure through which the policy measures of SP can be developed and refined.[38]

Objections/obstacles to Monetary Reform in the light of the likely reaction of global markets

Objections to Monetary Reform proposals such as *Creating New Money* have been outlined in the previous chapter. We now need to consider them more specifically in the light of the influence global markets could have on any government considering their *unilateral national* implementation.

(a)   As already mentioned, the relatively strong influence of global markets on government policy has given rise to a political monoculture in which political parties of whatever colour, once they come to govern, feel they have little or no choice but to conform to extremely narrow business and market-friendly parameters of economic, environmental and social policy. Monetary Reform is not a proposal likely to fall within those parameters, particularly from the point of view of the commercial banks!

(b)   While it may be true to say that Monetary Reform, *once implemented*, may make a nation economically more competitive, a potentially significant risk lies in the period of time between its adoption as official party policy by any major party and the time of the policy's actual implementation. During that pre-implementation period, if the party concerned is either in power or seriously looks like it might soon be voted in at a forthcoming election, global markets will have had ample intervening time to express their disapproval by causing currency devaluation, inflation, unemployment, capital flight and so on. Global markets and the commercial banks are thus in a position to take strong pre-

---

[38] To view the latest provisional policy content of SP, please visit www.simpol.org and click on 'Policy Proposals'

emptive action against policies they dislike *even before* they've been implemented.

(c)   In connection with (b) above, public support for Monetary Reform which may have been painstakingly built up by campaigners over a number of years could quickly unravel as the public is made aware that its implementation is likely to cost jobs, threaten the nation's competitiveness, or to have other adverse effects, even if only short-term. The evaporation of public support could also be reinforced by media campaigns undertaken by the commercial banks who would argue that the imposition of Monetary Reform – and the consequent loss of their money creation subsidy - would cause them to become uncompetitive with their banking competitors in other countries, thus potentially causing a loss of jobs. Were such a scenario to occur, it might in turn cause any political party that had initially adopted Monetary Reform to promptly drop it from its manifesto or policy platform. In that case, the hopes for the implementation of Monetary Reform would have been dashed and much of the painstaking efforts of a long-fought campaign consequently wasted.

In these circumstances, campaigners for Monetary Reform should consider whether a policy to remove from the commercial banks the right to create money is likely even to be *considered* for adoption by any political party, let alone implemented by any government on a unilateral national basis. If they accept that it is unlikely, they may conclude that the Simultaneous Policy approach might offer the Monetary Reform movement a possible way forward which, as we shall later see, need not mean abandoning their efforts to campaign for the implementation of monetary reform on a unilateral basis.

Specific Arguments in Favour of Simultaneous Policy

The main argument in favour of Simultaneous Policy (SP) is essentially a negative one: that proposals such as Monetary Reform are unlikely to be implemented in any way *other* than by many, if not all, nations implementing them simultaneously for the various reasons already outlined.

Nevertheless, the specific arguments in favour of SP are that:

(a)   Simultaneous international action would remove the fear of governments, political parties, businesses and citizens being first to 'go it alone'. It would therefore remove the possibility that capital markets or the commercial banks could in any way retaliate or take pre-emptive action to thwart its implementation. It would thus make the *adoption* of SP by governments or politicians risk-free insofar as implementation would only occur simultaneously: i.e. only when all or sufficient nations do likewise. In this way, the argument corporations commonly put forward that socially or environmentally favourable policies or higher taxes will make them uncompetitive with corporations in other countries would be completely obliterated. In the case of Monetary Reform, for example, commercial banks could no longer claim 'uncompetitiveness' as a valid objection and could not base any defensive lobbying on that argument nor on any threat that the policy would risk a loss of jobs. In removing these key obstacles and objections, SP would thus represent a powerful consensus-building strategy and one which would not risk any unraveling of public support. As more and more citizens, political parties and nations adopted SP, the pressure on the remainder would steadily increase towards a time when sufficient nations had adopted and implementation could proceed.

(b)   Since SP is a *'future policy'*, i.e. since the specific policy measures it would include would be implemented only on a simultaneous basis at some point in the future, the *current policies* of governments, politicians and political parties would be completely unaffected and they would not therefore need to change their existing policies or platforms if they decided to adopt SP. This means that, as a general principle, SP would be adoptable by virtually any political party of any colour since it presents politicians with no political risk and allows them to pursue their current policies until such time as all or sufficient nations had adopted SP.

(c)   Although many organisations that constitute the global justice movement do not yet appear to recognise it, many of the reforms they advocate fall to a greater or lesser extent into the SP category of policies likely to require simultaneous rather than unilateral implementation. Once this is fully recognised, however, campaigners of all kinds world-wide would be able to bring their various policy proposals under the single umbrella of SP, thus taking advantage of a common process for harmonising those demands and for getting them implemented. SP could therefore represent an effective vehicle for harmonising and implementing a multi-issue political agenda at the global level.

(d)   The number of votes needed to obtain the adoption of SP by the major political parties in many countries need not be large. This is because in countries with 'first-past-the-post' electoral systems, ISPO only needs to attract sufficient SP adopters to hold the critical balance of power between the two main parties in order for the adoption of SP by one or both main parties to become likely. As the U.S. Presidential election held in 2000 demonstrated, that critical balance can be extremely small indeed. So although the target of getting all or sufficient nations to adopt SP may at first appear a hopelessly ambitious task, the number of adopting citizens required may actually be much smaller than at first imagined.

(e)   SP potentially offers an entirely new electoral alternative likely to appeal to people across the political spectrum.[39] However, by not being a political party, ISPO has the additional yet critical advantage of having the potential to attract the support of previously apathetic or protest voters who have become disillusioned with party politics. With an

---

[39] As an example of SP's cross-party appeal, SP has been commented upon favourably by former Members of Parliament from both the UK Labour and Conservative parties, as well as by parliamentarians from other parties and countries.

increasing number of seats and elections being won or lost on fine margins, the re-entry of these voters into the electoral process as adopters of SP could become a decisive factor.

(f) SP could be a very viable strategy for overcoming the problem of corporate funding in politics – another factor likely to prevent the adoption of policies such as Monetary Reform. The 'carrot and stick' proposition described earlier is potentially capable of placing politicians in a position where financial inducements to act in corporate interests could at last be outweighed by the fear of losing their seats to candidates that have adopted SP.

(g) Since the atrocities of September 11th 2001, the tolerance of state authorities to street protest or to other forms of protest has become extremely low. Since SP would operate *through* existing political systems it does not depend on any form of protest but only on the continued upholding of citizens' right to vote. Unlike most other NGOs, ISPO could not therefore be accused of being undemocratic, in any way disruptive or of refusing to engage in established political processes.[40] However, this is not to suggest that non-violent protest represents an inappropriate form of action. Indeed, protest is surely vital if world problems are to be brought to wider public attention. But the key point is that, since SP does not *depend* on protest nor on conventional lobbying, it offers the Global Justice Movement an entirely complementary and potentially highly effective means of pursuing its political objectives.

---

[40] NGOs are already under threat from the U.S. Government and corporate-funded think-tanks such as the American Enterprise Institute (AEI). See for example Naomi Klein's article in the Globe and Mail, June 20th 2003, *Bush to NGOs: Watch Your Mouths* in which the AEI is quoted as saying that "The extraordinary growth of advocacy NGOs in liberal democracies has the potential to undermine the sovereignty of constitutional democracies".

Arguments Against Simultaneous Policy and Potential Responses to them

The most common objections to the SP approach and responses to them are as follows:[41]

a) **The prospect of expecting all, or virtually all, nations to do *anything*, let alone to simultaneously implement a complex range of measures such as SP, seems completely unrealistic.**

It is accepted that this is a valid concern. However, the key question is whether, in the circumstances, unilateral implementation is more or less realistic than simultaneous implementation. How realistic is it, after all, to expect a single or a restricted group of nations to unilaterally implement policies which are likely to provoke adverse capital market reactions and which are thus *against* their own interests? While the achievement of SP may admittedly appear highly ambitious, logically it is difficult to conceive of other ways in which such policies could be implemented.

If, on the other hand, one were to imagine that ISPO, with the support of the global justice movement, had been able to secure the adoption of SP by the EU, the USA and Japan, the prospect of all or virtually all other countries falling into line seems not that hard to imagine. Furthermore, as the world economic, social and environmental predicament worsens over the coming years, as regrettably seems inevitable, the pressure on politicians and businesses to support the SP approach will become steadily greater. For although SP may today appear to global elites to be thoroughly undesirable, it may, by then, appear very desirable indeed. Because when circumstances eventually become dire and a

---

[41] For a more comprehensive discussion of potential objections and responses to them, see the FAQ page of the SP website at www.simpol.org.

continuance of the status quo seems likely only to lead to disaster, for politicians and corporate interests to contemplate not cooperating to support the implementation of SP may by then have become as unthinkable as the idea of them not competing is today. By that time, it would potentially have become in virtually everyone's best interests to cooperate in implementing SP.

b)   **Is it really necessary to get ALL nations to adopt SP before implementation could proceed? Surely, that's never going to happen.**

The adoption of SP by *all* nations is *not* strictly necessary but it is clear that, for implementation to proceed in a secure manner, the adoption at least by *sufficient* nations would be required to avoid any significant risk of 'free-riding' by non-adopting nations. Furthermore, the definition as to what number of nations would be regarded as being "sufficient" is likely to depend on which specific SP policy measure is being considered. For Monetary Reform, for example, "sufficient" may be likely to mean all nations that could be expected to provide a reasonable domicile for the commercial banks and financial centres. In the case of the dismantling of all nuclear weapons, on the other hand, it may only require all those nations who possess, or are suspected of possessing, such weapons. In the end, however, the definition of what constitutes "sufficient nations" will be whatever number of nations are needed for all to feel adequately secure for implementation to proceed.

The important point to note, therefore, is that the SP criteria of "all, or virtually all, nations" is not to be understood as a condition 'written in stone' but rather as a *consensus-building strategy*; a way of removing key objections and thus persuading citizens, organisations and governments to say "yes" to such policies instead of "no".

c)   **The Kyoto Protocol still went ahead without the support of the USA, so does this not demonstrate that there is no need for ALL or sufficient nations to implement policies simultaneously?**

A key reason for the Kyoto Protocol being implemented by the international community without the participation of the USA is likely to be because the present provisions of the Protocol are so mild.[42] That being the case, the loss of competitive advantage likely to be suffered by those nations proceeding with the Protocol is not likely to be significant compared to nations such as the United States who did not proceed with it. But were the provisions of the Protocol to require *much more stringent* emissions reductions – as would be needed if a really significant impact on global warming is to be achieved – it is unlikely that any major nation would be willing to proceed unless all did likewise because the significant additional costs their industries would have to bear compared to those of nations not participating would not be economically sustainable: the competitive disadvantage would simply be too great. Therefore, it may be strictly true to say that such policies need not require simultaneous implementation. But in that case, their provisions will be so mild and ineffective as to be of highly questionable value. So, if we are to have international agreements that have a *really significant* effect on the environmental or economic problems they're supposed to solve, we are unlikely to get them unless all, or virtually all, nations implement them simultaneously. Hence the potential value of the proposed SP process.

---

[42] The provisions of the Kyoto Protocol call for a reduction in emissions to a level 5% below those recorded in 1990. However, most climate experts suggest that a 50-60% reduction is needed if a significant impact on global warming is to be made.

d) **If all nations have to implement a reform simultaneously, that will be used by corporate interests and national governments as a reason to do nothing, or at least to cause delay.**

Given common experience with today's efforts at international treaty-making, this objection appears extremely valid. However, there are two reasons for questioning it:

(i) Firstly, in countries where elections are held, it would be the adoption of SP *by individual citizens* and their pledge to vote for ANY politician or party who also adopts SP which drives the process. After all, politicians will not generally adopt SP out of their own volition; they will do so *only because their electoral success would have become dependent on it.* Citizens, through their adoption of SP, would therefore have the potential to lead governments, rather than the other way round. Thus, in countries where elections are held, it would not be governments or politicians who would be the key actors; it would be *citizens themselves.* As such, under the SP process, there is really no possibility for national governments to delay, only of citizen adopters doing so. But since the implementation of SP is chiefly designed to *benefit* citizens (rather than corporations, bankers or financiers), there is no reason to suppose that citizens *would* delay. Indeed, it is suggested that, far from delaying, the contrary is more likely to be the case.

Essentially, therefore, there is less reason to expect delay with SP than under the present system of government-led international treaty-making which, because of the fear of first-mover disadvantage, is in any case fraught with plausible excuses for delay or outright refusal. SP, on the other hand, would not only remove those excuses, it would put citizens in control of the process. This would potentially be all the more valid since, without the cooperation of the USA, little is likely to be achieved and, as we have seen, SP provides citizens with a powerful tool which allows them to ensure their respective governments – including the USA - comply.

(ii)   It should also be remembered that SP allows for a new, yet critical distinction to be made between two fundamentally different categories of policy. On the one hand, there are those policies, the unilateral implementation of which would be likely to have a *negative* impact on a nation's competitiveness, capital markets, etc. These policies would fall into the SP category. On the other, there are those policies likely to have a neutral or even a *positive* impact on a nation's competitiveness if implemented unilaterally.

The SP approach would naturally apply only to those likely to have a *negative* impact. All policies having a neutral or positive impact would, of course, be pursued by each nation independently and unilaterally and those policies would therefore have nothing to do with SP. After all, nations will not want to delay implementing policies likely to have a *positive* impact on their competitiveness because if they waited for others they'd only *lose* their competitive advantage! By the same token, it is wholly unrealistic to expect nations to unilaterally implement policies thought likely to have a *negative* impact on their competitiveness. In those cases SP might clearly offer a more realistic, practical and speedier way forward.

Furthermore, making a clearer distinction between these two policy categories and properly considering to which category each reform proposal belongs would be likely to result in the global justice movement arriving at a far more coherent strategy for seeking the implementation of policies in *both* categories. Those in the former (negative) category could be pursued by the global justice movement under the SP approach in conjunction with ISPO; those in the latter (positive) category could be pursued for unilateral national implementation by the usual methods. Making this distinction, and thus selecting the appropriate implementation strategy, consequently makes the pursuance of both categories of policy mutually supportive while avoiding undue confusion and consequent delay.

e) **But what about some of the so-called 'Third World' countries whose governments are either corrupt dictatorships or heavily influenced by foreign corporate interests. How are those countries to be persuaded to adopt SP?**

As this question suggests, most such countries are maintained in this sorry state of affairs as a result of the interests of foreign – usually Western - corporations or governments. Logically, therefore, pressure will be most effective if applied firstly to the rich countries or corporations who are responsible for maintaining this state of abusive exploitation. If electorates in the rich countries, through their adoption of SP, can bring their political parties and governments to adopt SP, corrupt governments in developing countries whom they are supporting will similarly come under such pressure.

Furthermore, where specific corporations could be identified, adopters of SP in richer countries could apply additional pressure through consumer boycotts, insisting that the boycott would continue until the corporations concerned brought sufficient pressure to bear on the respective developing country governments to adopt SP. But this is not to underestimate the pressure that could be brought to bear on these governments by the peoples of those countries themselves. They too could join with adopters of SP in the richer countries to bring sufficient electoral or other appropriate pressure to bear on all governments to adopt SP.

Again, this scenario might appear unrealistic when judged harshly by the poor norms and standards we are so used to witnessing in the world of politics today. However, when seen as a *developing process* against the backdrop of a steadily deteriorating world situation, it is clear that by the time it came to persuading some corrupt developing country governments to adopt SP, very many politicians and some governments in Western democracies would likely *already* have adopted it. World public opinion would thus already be solidly supportive of SP and the public's associated standards and expectations would, by then, therefore likely be quite different to what they are today. In those changed circumstances, and with world problems developing towards crisis, Western governments and corporations would be under extreme pressure to bring corrupt governments into line. For by that time, maintaining the status quo may well no longer represent a viable or attractive option to them and the alternative of supporting an orderly transition to a cooperative world order, as SP would facilitate, may by then represent the only sensible alternative.

CHAPTER 4

AN ACTION PROGRAMME FOR MONETARY REFORM
By James Robertson and John Bunzl

In this concluding chapter we summarise the types of action needed to promote monetary reform, and the part the Simultaneous Policy campaign might play.

Chapters 1 and 2 made two things clear. First, worldwide pressure for monetary reform will continue to grow. Second, the international aspects of monetary reform are crucially important.

Monetary reform will involve a variety of changes – at national, local, international and global levels. These will include changes in the way official currencies are issued and managed to meet people's needs in a fair and efficient way. They will also include a growing role for complementary currencies and quasi-currencies issued by commercial and community organisations to meet the needs of their members; a greater plurality of currencies will be a feature of 21st-century economic life. In this book we have concentrated on reform of official currencies, as a reform much needed in its own right which the Simultaneous Policy approach described in Chapter 3 might help to implement.

As with other important reforms to redress injustice and the balance of power and wealth between richer and poorer people and nations, it is realistic to assume that in the rich countries the campaign for monetary reform will initially have to continue to be taken forward by committed individuals and non-governmental organisations (NGOs). In due course the campaign will probably attract increasing support from the small business sector, rural interests and other economic sectors badly served by the present system of money and finance. Thereafter, support from among mainstream politicians, political parties, government officials, financial experts and professional and academic economists, can be expected to grow, but only when they perceive that the balance of risk and reward is shifting in favour of monetary reform – encouraging them to learn what it is, and then to consider seriously the arguments for introducing it.

In assessing that risk, one factor politicians will have to take into account, as explained in the previous chapter, is whether the unilateral introduction of monetary reform could have a negative impact on their nation's competitiveness, capital markets, employment levels and so on. This assessment would therefore bring into play the question of whether a unilateral or simultaneous implementation approach would, when the time comes, seem most appropriate.

In the meantime, action by individuals and NGOs to promote monetary reform can take the following forms:

- Supporters and campaigning organisations in a particular country can promote it in their own country.
- Supporters and campaigning organisations in different countries can cooperate with one another to promote it in their countries.
- Supporters and campaigning organisations in different countries can cooperate to promote it for international and global currencies, like the euro and a future world currency.

Action by Supporters and Campaigning Organisations to Promote Monetary Reform in Their Own Country

There is a lot of important work to be done under this heading.

The first task is to spread understanding and stimulate public debate about the issues discussed in Chapters 1 and 2:

- how the present mainstream national money system creates new money;
- why the proposed monetary reform is needed to deal with the inefficiencies and injustices inherent in that;
- why it may be expected to achieve the seven important benefits listed in Chapter 1 (pp20-21);
- what changes the proposed reform will mean in practice;
- why it will be a natural next stage in the history of monetary development;
- why the principle underlying the proposal for national monetary reform will also guide us in dealing with the even more glaring faults and injustices of the existing *international* monetary system; and
- what to do about the widespread ignorance and avoidance of this subject among politicians, officials, professionals, media commentators and economists who should be concerned with it.

One aim must be to generate the pressure of political and public opinion to persuade ministers responsible for the national central bank and the Ministry of Finance (the Treasury in the UK)

- to publish estimates of the loss of potential public revenue and the special profits to commercial banks that result from the present way of creating new money;
- to explain what benefits, if any, to the national economy and society match these costs; and
- to say whether they accept that the proposed reform would result in the benefits listed in Chapter 1, and if not why not.

It will be equally important to persuade these public servants responsible for monetary policy to publish their best estimates of how much the countries that issue the main international reserve currencies (US dollar, euro, yen and sterling) profit from issuing them, at the expense of the rest of the world.

A second but closely connected task will involve explaining clearly why most of the stock arguments against monetary reform noted in Chapter 2 rely on misunderstanding, misinformation and special pleading on behalf of the banking industry and other beneficiaries of the present system.

There is no reason why this range of activities should not be undertaken by people working separately in their own countries. But cooperative support between people in different countries could help them to work more effectively.

Action by Supporters and Campaigning Organisations Co-operating to Promote Monetary Reform in One Another's Countries

There are, in fact, good reasons why people in different countries should try to help and support one another in the activities mentioned above. Prophets are not without honour, save in their own countries. Ideas and proposals promoted abroad often attract more interest than those that come from fellow citizens – just as businesses often value the views of outside consultants more highly than those of their own people.

People who support monetary reform in Britain are already in close contact with people who support it in other countries, especially in Europe and the USA, Canada, and other English-speaking countries. But we need to expand the existing exchange of information into more active joint campaigns.

As Chapter 2 mentioned, campaigning by internationally active NGOs to change the plainly unjust and economically inefficient international monetary system that now exists is bound to grow. As this happens, it will indirectly help to spread understanding of the need for comparable national reforms, thereby strengthening the efforts of national groups campaigning for those. The commonality of principle underlying both will increasingly encourage campaigners for national and international monetary reform to support each other.

Action by Supporters and Campaigners in Different Countries Co-operating to Promote International Monetary Reform

The campaign for international monetary reform will obviously have to be based on cooperation between NGOs from different countries.

That kind of cooperation is already strong between NGOs which participate in gatherings like the Johannesburg Summit of August 2002 and others held by the World Bank, World Trade Organisation, UN Environment Programme, Habitat, and so on. But up to now their cooperation has been more about resisting and reforming international trade and investment policies that damage the wellbeing of poorer peoples and the world's ecosystems, than about supporting basic international monetary reform. That needs to change. NGOs need to recognise that, valid and necessary though their existing campaigns are, if the present level of injustice and inefficiency continues to be built into the way the world's money system works, measures to improve world trade and investment for poorer countries, or to reduce their existing debt, will be of limited and short-term value.

The Simultaneous Policy Approach

So far as *global* monetary reform is concerned there is no question about the need for Simultaneous Policy. Reform can only be achieved by agreement between enough national governments with enough collective influence. Simultaneous Policy potentially provides citizens with a practical method for bringing their respective national governments to cooperate in that way. Doubt about whether monetary reformers should adopt the Simultaneous Policy approach is relevant only to monetary reform in individual countries - and in currency areas like the Eurozone.

There are good reasons for believing that, once introduced, monetary reform would improve, not damage, the overall international competitiveness of a country's economy as well as the general wellbeing of its people. In principle, therefore, a strong case could probably be made for many countries to introduce it unilaterally in advance of others. Economic analysis is needed to produce best estimates of the total costs and benefits that would arise from unilateral reform, e.g. in the UK.

In practice, however, it is realistic to recognise that the wealthy and powerful sectoral interests that benefit from the present system will continue to do everything they can to keep public and political opinion unconvinced by the case for reform or ignorant of it, while they emphasise the negative short-term impacts it could have on sectors like commercial banking. Against that opposition it will be difficult, and likely to take a long time, to achieve monetary reform in one or in a restricted group of countries only. And if the power of globally mobile sectoral interests is ultimately felt to be too great, unilateral implementation could even become an effective impossibility. That is the basic argument for Simultaneous Policy. But there is also a counter-argument, and an important question to be answered.

The counter-argument is that, starting virtually from scratch, it could be even more difficult and take an even longer time to develop a powerful worldwide Simultaneous Policy movement, then to get monetary reform included in its policy agenda, and then actually to achieve simultaneous monetary reform in enough important countries.

However, the response to that seems clear. Whichever approach is taken, unilateral or simultaneous, the achievement of monetary reform presents a challenging task, difficult to achieve in the immediate future. That means that, at least for the present, its supporters – like the supporters of many other reforms called for by the global justice movement - will be wise to consider going forward with *both* approaches.

But that prompts the important question: Will adopting the Simultaneous Policy mean suspending action to promote monetary reform in an individual country until it becomes possible to introduce it simultaneously in many? If the answer to that question were Yes, then most monetary reformers would no doubt be unwilling to adopt it. Fortunately the answer is No, for the present at least.

It has not yet been settled what specific policy measures, such as monetary reform, should be included in the Simultaneous Policy agenda. So the policy content of SP remains only provisional and tentative and is likely to remain so for some time. There are good reasons for this gradual and provisional approach. Firstly, it would be entirely undemocratic for ISPO irrevocably to fix its policy at an early stage because that would deny potential new members the opportunity to participate in developing it. Secondly, since we live in a changing world and since SP is likely to take some years to be achieved, any policies irrevocably fixed today could be out of date or inappropriate by the time SP came to be implemented.

What *is* clear today, however, is that SP would cover a *multi*-issue reform agenda. So adopting SP at this stage does not entail a commitment to adopt it for any specific measure. By adopting it provisionally, monetary reformers would simply be recognising the possibility that, when eventually almost enough support for monetary and other important reforms has built up in a number of countries to get them introduced, it could still be necessary to neutralise continuing fears about their possible effects on international competitiveness or capital markets. In other words, by adopting SP provisionally, monetary reformers would be hedging their bets in case, some time in the future, circumstances might favour introducing monetary reform simultaneously in different countries. At the same time, they would be joining with other supporters of the global justice movement who similarly recognise that many of the reforms they are calling for may, like monetary reform, ultimately require a simultaneous implementation approach. Meanwhile, for the present all those who had adopted SP, be they supporters of monetary or other reforms, will remain entirely free to campaign for the unilateral implementation of their respective proposals. Neither approach therefore excludes the other.

Provisionally adopting SP might also give opportunities to supporters of monetary reform to make new links with other monetary reformers around the world who have adopted it, and – perhaps more importantly - with people who have adopted SP to support other reforms, such as those put forward in the "Earth Emergency Call to Action" at the 2002 Johannesburg Summit (see Chapter 1, pp22). This could help to promote monetary reform, not just as a single issue which many people will continue to shy away from as complicated and abstruse, but as a key part of the integrated world-wide programme of political, social and economic reform that they recognise as necessary. ISPO could therefore provide a useful means for bringing monetary reform to the attention of other global justice campaigners, and helping to strengthen support for it.

This combined, twin-track, national and international approach would also seem to resonate positively with campaigners of all stripes, whether they favour global solutions that seek to make open markets more socially just or whether they seek global solutions to allow the prioritisation of the protection and rediversification of local economies i.e. 'localisation'.[43] For on the one hand, Simultaneous Policy's criterion of "all or sufficient nations acting simultaneously" clearly indicates a global level approach and yet, on the other, it clearly depends on the participation of each nation. So while SP will represent an important evolutionary step towards a form of global governance, it would equally bring a far greater degree of autonomy to each nation than exists at present, allowing each far greater freedom to solve national and local problems within SP's overarching, cooperative framework. SP's synthesis of global unity and national diversity could therefore offer potential common ground

---

[43] To give contrasting examples of these two approaches, for 'localisation', see *Localization – A Global Manifesto* by Colin Hines, Earthscan, 2000. For a global solutions approach, see *The Age of Consent – A Manifesto for a New World Order* by George Monbiot, Flamingo, 2003.

between both the 'socially just, open markets' camp and the 'localisation' camp. Indeed, 'localisation' is often wrongly perceived by its detractors as a withdrawal from international cooperation in favour of purely isolationist, national or local solutions. In fact, however, genuine 'localisers' recognise that a high level of international cooperation is also required for many key localisation policies to be implemented and successfully maintained.

We conclude therefore that there is nothing to be lost, and possibly much to be gained, by supporters of monetary reform provisionally adopting SP at the present time. We believe the same is true for supporters of many other reforms and policy changes on which progress towards a more just, environmentally benign and economically efficient world society depends, but which powerful corporate interests claim would jeopardise the economic competitiveness of the national economy and their particular sector of it.

Simultaneous Policy Adoption Form
(Please do not tear this form out. Please photocopy instead)

I confirm my provisional adoption of the Simultaneous Policy (SP). By provisionally adopting SP I pledge to vote in future elections for ANY personally acceptable candidate who has provisionally adopted SP or to encourage my preferred candidate or party, if I have one, to provisionally adopt SP. If my country does not allow me to vote, I pledge to do what I can to influence my government to adopt SP.

I understand my adoption of SP is provisional because SP is a work-in-progress. My provisional adoption entitles me to join with other adopters in formulating SP's vital measures for global peace, justice, security and sustainability. I may revoke adoption of SP at any time by notifying the International Simultaneous Policy Organisation.

Last Name (Mr./Mrs/Miss/Ms)......................................

First Name...

Postal Address...

....

....

Post Code.....................Country................................

Email...

Nationality...

Telephone (optional)...

Fax (optional)..

Signed.................................Date........................

Please tick as appropriate:

□ I would like to become involved in campaigning for the adoption of SP

□ I am a member of these other NGOs (please list)

....

....

□ Please send me ...... copies of *"The Simultaneous Policy: An Insider's Guide to Saving Humanity and the Planet"* by John Bunzl. Prices per copy including postage and packing: UK£12.50 €23.00 US$20.00 C$32.00 A$38.00 Sfr.36.00 Dkr.170 Skr.210

Optional: I would like to make a donation to ISPO. I enclose cheque payable to "ISPO" for the book and/or donation in the sum of:
£...............................

Thank you!

International Simultaneous Policy Organisation
P.O. Box 26547, London SE3 7YT, UK

www.simpol.org   email: info@simpol.org

Tel: +44 (0)20-8464 4141   Fax: +44 (0)20-8460 2035

FURTHER READING and RESOURCES: MONETARY REFORM

David Boyle, *The Money Changers: currency reform from Aristotle to e-cash*, Earthscan, London, 2002.

Richard Douthwaite, *The Ecology of Money,* Schumacher Briefing No. 4, Green Books, 1999.

Richard Douthwaite, *Defense and the Dollar*, 2002 and Feasta, *Climate and Currency: Proposals for Global Monetary Reform*, 2002, prepared for the Johannesburg World Summit on Sustainable Development by Feasta – see under Contacts.

Thomas H. Greco, *Money: Understanding and Creating Alternatives to Legal Tender*, Chelsea Green Publishing, USA, 2001.

Romilly Greenhill and Ann Pettifor, *The United States as a HIPC (heavily indebted prosperous country) - how the poor are financing the rich*, New Economics Foundation, London, 2002.

Hazel Henderson, *Beyond Globalization: Shaping a Sustainable Global Economy,* Kumarian Press (for the New Economics Foundation), 1999.

Joseph Huber and James Robertson, "Creating New Money: A monetary reform for the information age", New Economics Foundation, London, 2000. www.neweconomics.org

Michael Hudson, *Super Imperialism: The Origin and Fundamentals of World Domination*, Pluto Press, 2003.

Frances Hutchinson, Mary Mellor and Wendy Olsen, *The Politics of Money: Towards Sustainability and Economic Democracy*, Pluto Press, 2002.

Margrit Kennedy, *Interest and Inflation Free Money: Creating an exchange medium that works for everybody and protects the earth*, New Society Publishers, USA.

Bernard Lietaer, *The Future of Money,* Random House, 2000.

Henry C K Liu, *US Dollar Hegemony Has Got To Go,* Asia Times Online Co Ltd, 2002.

Ann Pettifor (ed), *Real World Economic Outlook: the legacy of globalisation: debt and development,* Palgrave Macmillan, 2003.

Prosperity: Freedom from Debt Slavery, an informative monthly newsletter edited by Alistair McConnachie, Prosperity, 268 Bath Street, Glasgow G2 4JR – e-mail: admcc@admcc.freeserve.co.uk

Michael Rowbotham,
   The Grip of Death: A study of modern money, debt slavery and destructive economics, 1998, and
   Goodbye America! Globalisation, debt and the dollar empire, 2000,
both published by Jon Carpenter Publishing, Oxfordshire.

Schumacher Briefings Nos. 1, 4, 5 and 9 all deal with questions about money and the sharing of resources – information from Schumacher Society, The Create Centre, B-Bond Warehouse, Smeaton Road, Bristol BS1 6XN, England. www.schumacher.org.uk

Rodney Shakespeare and Peter Challen, *Seven Steps to Justice*, New European Publications, London, 2002.

Stephen Zarlenga, *The Lost Science of Money: The Mythology of Money – The Story of Power*, American Monetary Institute. www.monetary.org. Email: ami@taconic.net

ORGANISATIONS

Christian Council for Monetary Justice
Peter Challen   peter@southwark.org.uk

Committee on Monetary and Economic Reform (COMER)
www.comer.org
William Krehm   wkrehm@comer.org

FEASTA, the Foundation for the Economics of Sustainability
9 Lower Rathmines Road, Dublin 6, Ireland;
feasta@anu.ie
www.feasta.org

Forum for Stable Currencies
www.intraforum.net/money
Peter Challen   peter@southwark.org.uk
Sabine Kurjo McNeill   sabine@globalnet.co.uk

Lebensgarten Eco-Village, Steyerberg, Germany
International workshops on monetary reform
Profs. Declan and Margrit Kennedy   www.lebensgarten.de

New Economics Foundation
www.neweconomics.org
info@neweconomics.org

South African New Economics Foundation (SANE)
sane@sane.org.za
www.sane.org.za
Aart de Lange   ardl@iafrica.com
Margaret Legum   legum@mweb.co.za

Note: The books and organisations listed above will provide many more references for readers who wish to follow them up.

FURTHER READING and RESOURCES: SIMULTANEOUS POLICY

John Bunzl, *The Simultaneous Policy – An Insider's Guide to Saving Humanity and the Planet,* New European Publications, London 2001. Various short articles on SP can be downloaded directly from the 'Campaigning' page of the SP website www.simpol.org.

John Gray, *False Dawn – The Delusions of Global Capitalism,* Granta Books, London 1998.

Noreena Hertz, *The Silent Takeover – Global Capitalism and the Death of Democracy,* William Heinemann, London 2001.

Colin Hines, *Localization – A Global Manifesto,* Earthscan, London 2000.

Hans-Peter Martin & Harald Schumann, *The Global Trap – Globalization and the Assault on Democracy and Prosperity,* Zed Books, London 1997.

George Monbiot, *The Age of Consent – A Manifesto for a New World Order,* Flamingo, London 2003.

Layna Mosley, *Global Capital and National Governments,* Cambridge University Press, Cambridge, 2003.

ORGANISATIONS

International Simultaneous Policy Organisation (ISPO)
P.O. Box 26547, London SE3 7YT, UK
www.simpol.org   info@simpol.org

Book Ordering Information

To order copies of James Robertson's *Creating New Money*, co-written with Joseph Huber, please contact the New Economics Foundation, 3 Jonathan Street, London SE11 5NH, UK. Email: info@neweconomics.org. Tel. 020-7820 6300.

To order John Bunzl's *The Simultaneous Policy*, or for further copies of this book or others in the ISPO *Making it Happen!* series, please contact the International Simultaneous Policy Organisation, P.O. Box 26547, London SE3 7YT, UK. Email: info@simpol.org. Tel. 020-8464 4141.

Praise for Simultaneous Policy

"I thought your proposal was an elegant idea of how change could occur. It reflects the core ideas of how to create consensus around change. This is the biggest challenge that we have"
Ed Mayo. Former Exec. Director, New Economics Foundation

"It's ambitious and provocative. Can it work? Certainly worth a serious try."
Noam Chomsky

"With his concept of Simultaneous Policy, John Bunzl delivers an important piece in the puzzle that governments around the world can use to resolve the pressures of increasingly integrated markets. ... It is, perhaps, one of the few workable solutions to bridging the sustainability gap."
Matthias Hoepfl *Politische Oekologie*, Munich, Germany

"...provocative and potentially transformative. There are ideas here that could change the world."
Prof. Charles Derber Dept. of Sociology, Boston College, MA, USA.